INSIGHT

Daniel Benjamin

mc Marshall Cavendish
Benchmark
New York

Other Marshall Cavendish Offices:
Marshall Cavendish International (Asia) Private Limited, 1 New Industrial Road, Singapore 536196 • Marshall Cavendish International (Thailand) Co Ltd. 253 Asoke, 12th Flr, Sukhumvit 21 Road, Klongtoey Nua, Wattana, Bangkok 10110, Thailand • Marshall Cavendish (Malaysia) Sdn Bhd, Times Subang, Lot 46, Subang Hi-Tech Industrial Park, Batu Tiga, 40000 Shah Alam, Selangor Darul Ehsan, Malaysia

Marshall Cavendish is a trademark of Times Publishing Limited

All websites were available and accurate when this book was sent to press.

Library of Congress Cataloging-in-Publication Data

Elish, Dan.
Insight / by Daniel Benjamin.
   p. cm. — (Green cars)
Summary: "Provides information on the hybrid technology used in the Insight, and discusses how the green movement is affecting the auto industry"— Provided by publisher.
Includes bibliographical references and index.
ISBN 978-1-60870-010-3
1. Insight automobile — Juvenile literature. 2. Hybrid electric cars — Juvenile literature. I. Title.
TL215.I56E45 2011
629.22'93 — dc22
   2009041716

Editor: Megan Comerford
Publisher: Michelle Bisson
Art Director: Anahid Hamparian
Series Designer: Daniel Roode

Illustrations on pp. 18–19 by Alanna Ranellone

Photo research by Connie Gardner

Cover photo by: Ron Kimball/www.kimballstock.com

The photographs in this book are used by permission and through the courtesy of:
Ron Kimball/www.kimballstock.com: 9, 24; Getty Images: Toru Yamanaka, 17,22; Nicholas Ratzenback, 27; Klyoshi Oto, 30; Yoshikazu Tsuno, 32, 37; William West, 41; AP Photo: Nick Ut, 12; Alamy: izmostock, 14; Martin Goddard, 40.

Printed in Malaysia (T)
135642

Contents

Introduction

Most cars in the world run on gasoline, and some cars use more gas than others. Gasoline is made from petroleum, or crude oil, which is a liquid buried deep in the earth. Petroleum formed naturally from the **decomposed** and **compressed** remains of tiny **organisms** that lived millions of years ago. Humans drill deep into the earth to take the oil out.

However, the amount of oil in the world is limited. The more we take out of the ground now, the less there will be in the future, and it will eventually run out. Taking it out of the ground is expensive and damages the **environment**.

Also, when oil and the products made from oil (gasoline, engine oil, heating oil, and diesel fuel) are burned, they give off pollution in the form of gases that damage the **atmosphere**. The carbon dioxide (CO_2) that gasoline-burning engines give off is one of the major causes of **global warming**.

Carbon dioxide is a **greenhouse gas**. Like the glass panes of a greenhouse, the gas traps heat. The build-up of carbon dioxide in the atmosphere, scientists warn, is keeping Earth's heat from escaping into space. As a result, the planet is warming up.

In the United States, about 90 percent of the greenhouse gases we produce is from burning oil, gasoline, and coal. One-third of this comes from the engines that power the vehicles we use to move people and objects around. If we do not stop this global warming, life on Earth could begin to get very uncomfortable.

The problem is not just that temperatures might rise a bit. A warming atmosphere could melt the ice of the Arctic and Antarctic, raise the level of water in the seas, and change the **climate** of many places on Earth. Animals unable to adjust to the new conditions might become extinct (die out). Plants and crops might no longer be able to grow where people need them. Many islands, low-lying countries, and communities along the coasts of all the continents might disappear into the sea.

Doesn't sound so good, does it? These problems are why many people are interested in **alternative fuels** that can power our cars and other engines with less or no pollution.

Now that you know that oil is made from living things that died a long time ago, it should be no surprise that people are making oil from live plants to power their cars. This fuel, called *biodiesel*, can be made from soybean oil, canola oil, sunflowers, and other plants. Biodiesel is similar to the vegetable oil used for cooking. Some people gather or buy this used oil from restaurants and use it to power their cars. The engines in these cars have to be modified, or changed, in order to burn this oil correctly.

Another popular way to power cars is with batteries. Modern batteries are being made to be so powerful that some cars use them in combination with gas engines; this system is called *hybrid technology*. Hybrid cars have a gas engine and an electric motor. The electric motor usually takes over when the car runs at low speeds or when it stops.

Many auto engineers are designing electric cars that run only on batteries. Until recently, too many batteries were needed to make this an **efficient** technology. But there have been important advances in battery technology.

Another form of alternative energy for cars is the hydrogen **fuel cell**, which gives off power when the hydrogen and oxygen in the fuel cell are combined. If we are to start driving hydrogen-powered cars, however, hydrogen fueling stations would have to be as common along U.S. roads and highways as gas stations are today.

Oil is a limited resource, costs a lot to extract, pollutes the land, air, and water, and forces most countries to rely on the few nations that have a plentiful supply of it. If the world wants to become a cleaner, safer place, developing alternative fuels to power at least some of our vehicles is extremely important.

The Insight was the first mass-produced hybrid car to hit the U.S. market. It was not an immediate success. However, people are becoming more aware of global warming and more concerned about the price of gas. So, the Insight is growing in popularity.

Drivers like the Insight because it produces fewer harmful emissions than most cars. An electric motor provides some of the Insight's power, so drivers do not have to fill the gas tank as often as they would if they drove a regular car. This saves money at the gas pump.